BOOM TOWN

BOOM TOWN

Diane Glancy

Black Hat Press

Published by Black Hat Press
Box 12, Goodhue, Minnesota 55027
Books may be ordered from the above address
Cover photo: *Fish Houses*, oil on canvas, mounted on masonite.
Undated. By Helen Henton. From the Collection of the Minnesota
Historical Society.

Author's photo © 1997 Jane Katz

ISBN:1-887649-11-5

Acknowledgment to *Metis a feminist quarterly* for "A Woman
Sweeping"; *Phase and Cycle* for "Slipping into What Will Hold
Onto"; *Mankato Poetry Review* for "Mt. Scott, Southwest Okla-
homa"; *Sidewalks* for "Quake at Lake Superior," "Ice-Fishing
Houses"; *Midwest Quarterly, Great Plains Issue*, for "Mostly It
Was Arid There before the Windmill"; *Rain Dog Review* for
"Tableland"; *Lightning & Ash* for "All Right Write Your Book";
ArtWord Quarterly for "The Pine Cones Have Gone Mad," "A
Condensation During Flight," "Grand Portage Casino"; *Black
River Review* for "The Rain Stealer"; *Image, a Journal of Art &
Religion* for "Front Rank"; *Teacup* for "The Actors"; *The Lucid
Stone* for "Boom Town," "Kissing the Sun"; *Fergus Falls* for "A
Lake Swimming Beneath," "A Quick Rise from Icewater," "A
Forecast of Snowfields, Wind."

Acknowledgment to the Minnesota Humanities Commission for
subvention.

I thank the Minnesota Private College Research Foundation with
funds provided by the Blandin Foundation of Grand Rapids, Min-
nesota, for supporting a project during which some of these po-
ems were written.

I also thank the Playwrights' Center for a Many Voices Fellow-
ship during which "A Share of the Stair" was written.

Gratefulness to Jim Turnure.

And lastly, I thank Beverly Voldseth of Black Hat Press and The Loft.

Out of whose womb came the ice?
Job 38:29

OTHER BOOKS BY DIANE GLANCY

NOVELS

Pushing the Bear
The Only Piece of Furniture in the House

SHORT STORIES

Monkey Secret
Firesticks
Trigger Dance

ESSAYS

The West Pole
Claiming Breath

DRAMA

War Cries

POETRY

Lone Dog's Winter Count
Iron Woman
Offering
One Age in a Dream

Contents

Consider a moment the shoreline open
to the water if you look at it that way
the bait shops on northern shores
the jagged edge of water just under air.

Cleared as Pines

I came from Oklahoma where boom towns were the sudden settlements that grew up overnight around the oil rigs, and disappeared just as quickly.

When I moved to Minnesota and saw the ice-fishing houses sitting on the frozen lakes in winter and stored along the North Shore in summer, the idea, *boom town,* returned.

As I began to write about Minnesota and the cold, the concept of *boom town* opened to other possibilities. A *boom town* became the idea of love and the complications of relationships with families and spouse. A *boom town* could be a marriage. It could be the metaphor for the disparities of casino, the barracks in Germany, our language, those spurts of renewal in the middle of the journey, our lives, and even our civilization.

I wanted to work with the changing concepts of *boom town* I found along the road, and the readjustments which are a necessary part of thinking. I need to see from different ways. I like to know that objects can be redefined by setting and circumstance, and terms from history can be reused.

I wanted to work with how the meaning of words such as *line* and *stage,* for instance, vary according to their juxtaposition to other words such as *lake* and *theater.*

I like configurations of placements. The changing meaning of language. The unreliability of it. The paradox of its strength.

But there were further developments. Opposites such as glacier and volcano—and other images, ice-fishing houses and the abstraction of drama, which seemed to have nothing in common, could work together.

The tightness of air on the water began to loosen. I could feel the scenes in a drama between the bordertowns of water/ice and air.

I looked at the poems as ice-fishing houses standing on a flooring which is subject to change, migrating from the ice to the shore and back again. I wanted my words to be openings drilled through the ice into the water. I wanted an ice-fishing village of a book.

I wanted to incorporate words like little towns I passed on the roads of Minnesota, Montana, Wyoming, Oklahoma, and even Washington, D.C.

I wanted to explore the passing.

I have always lived in the Great Plains, the middle corridor of America. From Oklahoma to Minnesota. The land. The air. The trees here and there. The moving landscape in my peripheral vision as I drive. The elliptical lines of words. That's where imagery moves. Just off to the side. "The flagfield of them (the trees) waving a shore / overrun its edge along the sky" (from *Overland Pass*). I think it's the voices of the Great Plains that form my work. The heat and cold. The horsetanks. The lakes and man-made ponds. The sleet and snow that move like a herd across the land. The ceremonies of the season. The ordinary endurance.

I also wanted to discover the moments of transcendence—"until frozen over you drive across it" (from *A Quick Rise from Icewater*)—which, in my experience, was a 2 1/2 mile plowed ice-road I drove across on Lake Superior from the shore to a small inhabited island in winter. There was something ethereal in the realization that ice was between my car and 300 feet of water in the lake. There was something "other" in the windsled that waited on the other shore, a custom boat with a small airplane engine mounted in it, an airplane wheel at the prow, rudders at the stern. It was a boat made to cross the ice, but when the ice begins to break up, as boom towns do, and you could find yourself sinking, you want your words like a windsled which will float.

BOOM TOWN

The Pine Cones Have Gone Mad

They dig holes in the pine needle forest, bury squirrels for winter, dig them up long afterwards in nights that linger like regret. We could have done better, could have ordered our lives before they went haywire, jumped like coils from bedsprings. We drive on the highway like someone who should not be out of class, call like squirrels under forest floors. We would lift the planks for them but the pine cones hold grenades. Their shingled coats impenetrable. We can never go back to schools where we went, houses where we lived, can never get back the pine-cone heart.

All Right Write Your Book about Your Creative Process
You Talk about All the Time

for Maria Irene Fornes

I'd like to have it between covers
bound
how you bring in elements of distraction
in drama you feel anger but then rage
and maybe desire and how the development
of diversities and otherness is making
what we have here on earth
a little less flat
you want to take a step or maybe leap
to unlimit the tight rope around you
we have to have our space
whyshould we want to interlope
we're more like Five Mile Island
in Lake Superior
yes let me sit there and open
the system of how we work the methods
that are part of the working which works
the ability to function with images
rather than words or ideas
how if reading a script
you said *lookup*
and the actress would have trouble
and you would say *see the angels up there*
and afterwards she could lookup
rather don't set up a rigid way
of thinking but the creative mind approaches
the open ended work you do
is how you know this's native land by
nomenclature
on your own
slung between Oklahoma and Minnesota
Kansas and Missouri
not one of them not an Indian name
for a while your creative process
is under the surface
when writing is *uptosnuff*
from the moment we let other things come

with their buckets
our kinetic energies unload
becoming the boom town which drama is
the force within you
of the human sort.

The Shade of a Weedy Airfield

A string of fish thread-lined
to a north-shore smokehouse
the morning uncased
as fog over the bay
curled at the top in waves
you know the spirit speaks
to the given land
all weedy as air
coming to a revision of laps
you know when it speaks
but you can't understand.

A Woman Sweeping

I have seen this yard
a hundred times.
The air cooling the doorway.
The cat looking at the bird.
The bird at the cat.
A child crossing the yard.
The bird flying away.
It's the hundredth record
all new and raw.
The ground still a winter brown.
Old leaves raking it.
The pigeons taking grass-stalks
for their nest.
The cat who doesn't move
in this warm spell
while she stares at another bird.
The bush blossom-full.
Pigeons fly from the roof
to the yard and back again.
This early spring
before winter returns
or the phone rings.
Birch logs not burned in winter
stacked against the house.
Overhead a plane steps to the sky.
On the street the mere rejoicing
of a car.
The weed clumps.
The white shape of the house
across the drive.
The sun's light enlarging it.
The thought of some gray shore
waiting in summer.
The waves like flaps of pigeon wings.

Quake at Lake Superior

The waves
    breaking

on the rocks
    lift

the summer
    fog

the dockyard
    voices

the tourist
    cabins

tamaracks
    you

see the
    rusted

anchors of
    abandoned

stars the
    sound

of waves
    in trem-

ors of the
    heart.

Ice-Fishing Houses

Stacked on the
    shore a

sudden settle-
    ment of

cloudheads
    lifting

skyward Pigeon
    Creek

Great Falls
    tarpaper

winging toward
    afternoon.

Grand Portage Casino

Go to the sea, and cast a hook, and take up the fish that
first comes up; and when you have opened his mouth,
you will find a piece of money.

Matthew 17:27

Nothing known but the lake tossing waves or as much of them as were in Galilee with only the wind stirring the underness of trees without motorboats or freighters. Only countfulness at Grand Portage Casino in a bay of Lake Superior. The steady slap of motion. This gift from the sea.

The Rain Stealer

The woman who laps the lake
is good
she says
the coldness the sandiness
and rockiness along the base
the lichen on the cliffs
she holds her tongue into
where the steep part makes a taste of it
the whole place.

Sermon to the Rocks That Migrate on the Shore

The spots in the rock reminded him of the different size of birds
he said. As we talked of the rocks we collected around the table.
Told stories of them. That night in the cabin. Quartz specks in
granite called above the water. The unclaimed rocks remained on
the table. All night they cried to be chosen. Not returned to the
shore. A few pebbles among the many under the sky lifting its
short sightedness from the invisible skaters on the morning lake.
Their blade-marks moving shoreward always toward us. Toward
the crowd of trees cut through. The mov't of low clouds. A gla-
cier of quartz specks above the call of air. Their tongues forming
shades of light. I talked to the unwanted rocks as I tossed them
back to the shore. With stories telling them one day they would
all be in heaven. One day their voices would form the very core
of God. They would speak their maker's praise. The rocks chuck-
led as they landed. They did. I heard them from their different
flights.

The Stage

In this last
    before

the after-
    grounds

sideways in
    the

crevice
    wave-

ward and
    battle-

ford you
    hear

the inver-
    sions

overlap some
    things

like rust
    can

hardly be des-
    troyed.

United States Holocaust Memorial Museum
Washington, D.C.

. . . the sudden barracks,
the piles of hair and shoes,
the prisoners' suits and faded stripes,
whole names that disappeared.

You look for what will halt
the extraction of behavior to be explained
in words that could sever you from this
what terms of language could reach
and suck out
if events could be gassed and die
but the answers are not soon
if you could understand the matter of degree
from unkindness to hate
to expose the bald head of the human heart
at its twisted worst
at its gestapo in the root of mind
a gusher worse than the root of evil
to know any one of us if driven far enough
could be part
and must remember the antidote
which is the clean whole air of knowledge
the limit of divining what should be done
with the undesirable
some shelving God to the ineffectual
and maybe not even there
the guilt shame the curiosity you reach
when you redefine the head
to see if you could call God back
give Him another chance
He who is mighty and just and forgiving
who speaks with a voice
soft and still as hair.

Arrival of the Jugglers, 1926, Paul Klee,
The Phillips Collection, Washington, D.C.

The sudden gushers
    tented to

the barest ground
    windy

with rainstorm
    the woman

in the museum
    who keeps

asking the
    children

questions there
    are no

answers for but
    hers

she tries to
    draw from

the children
    what is

in her mind not
    theirs

you remember
    in school

you said what
    the teach-

ers didn't want
    to hear

and how
　　they

shushed you
　　soon

you grew
　　bored

you might
　　have

raised the
　　air

invisible as
　　jugglers

lifting
　　balls

and bowling
　　pins

the heaviness
　　of the

whole universe
　　rest-

ing on your
　　hand.

Overland Pass

The trees weighted their invisibility
with layers of the sky fretting.

A few trees holding their belief.
But mostly under them the overflown lake

permanently outwatered.
It was you and I

trees that stood in loose water a while.
The flagfield of them waving a shore

overrun its edge along the sky
and stood stripless as leaves.

We seemed to have passed there on the road
an ark with a commandment to believe.

Developing trees in their role of them
maybe underland.

The roving grasses inhabiting
the sky's invasion.

It was an affirming afterfix
much of which had been lost.

But in the crust of atmosphere it appears
in the invisible trees

an ascension
not unbelievable this late in the game.

Tourist

Where you've come
is a roadside cafe
in the shape of a fish

you see along the road
a turnaround
agreeing for once

you get out of the car
a little table of hurt
the going over it

til noontime
here someone *knowssomething*
you signup

even if he goes his way
you can walk
as in winter

when you step onto
the solid field of a lake
above the fish.

Slipping into What Will Hold Onto

The boomtown's an open space
a weeding out's what moving does
when you're ready
to be a room
boxed for transport
you'll see something and something
different'll come to you
how circumstances are little
windows with curtains blowing possibilities
as the art of human making
its drafts easing into full season
until it's without
its weight that holds it in the room.

A Share of the Stair

(or As I'm Talking I'm Becoming
What I Say)

> *No one knows what they are about or,*
> *for that matter, where they came from.*
> "The Visitation"
> Tom Whalen

Memory is a moraine. A little clutter of stones the glacier left when it retreated.

I look through the rubble. In 1951 when I was ten, my family came to Minnesota for a vacation. It must have taken a long time. Up through Missouri, Iowa, and nearly through Minnesota past Brainerd somewhere around Itasca.

I can't remember and my parents are dead. So I look at the Minnesota map.

St. Cloud. Brainerd. Baxter. Staples. Wadena. Sebeka. Fish Hook Lake. Potato Lake. Maybe Lake George. At least I remember Paul Bunyon. And Itasca, Headwaters of the Mississippi River.

In those days when there were narrow two-lane highways, it was hard to get around the slower traffic. It was hard to get through the towns.

To come all that way north must have taken years. To wind through Minneapolis and St. Paul when there were no bypasses. To drive nearly to Canada.

I don't know the place we stayed. I'll give it a name. *The Star of the North Sky Resort.*

You see memories are shape-changers moving among us. So we create when we remember. My mother and father and brother would name it differently.

I think there were pine trees. The dock and rowboat in the vaca-

18

tion waters of our family landscape. My father maybe fishing. My mother cooking in the cabin with its checked tablecloth. What a vacation for her. More of the same.

I remember a horse that chased me in the corral at *The Star of the North Sky Resort*. I remember running behind a tree and the two boys who were ranch hands well they laughed when I ran. They were probably eighteen and I was ten and wanted not to be laughed at by older boys when I was afraid of a horse.

But that summer of 1951, the Kaw River flooded the stockyards in Kansas City where my father worked and they called my dad back to Missouri. We loaded the car again and drove south through Minnesota, through Iowa to Kansas City, just a few days after we arrived.

That was my beginning in Minnesota to be followed nearly 40 years later when I moved to St. Paul.

This is my explaining ceremony.

I'm becoming the story I say. Otherwise nothingness scatters the pebbles with its horse's feet.

There's something I feel I have to get it right. Though there is no right to get. We all see in our own way and meaning is a moraine of possibilities.

You know I don't think my greatgrandfather knew what he was doing. Running from Indian Territory after he got in trouble. Leaving us without a name or a past. Other than the trouble he got in. Other than we know he had to run.

There's a blankness in my tribal memory. Like knowing there used to be a mountain in Minnesota. Until the glacier pushed it flat.

Even if the past was trouble and loss. You can feel the frozen history you don't remember. You pick things up. Push them along. Leave them in retreat.

But maybe the Mississippi would have gone another way. And maybe I would not have been part of the new, acculturated vacation-taking Indians without a past.

I would not have been a *leftout* of the white world and the Indian.

I remember the vacation in Minnesota cut short. An over-sized ox. An undersized river. Out of proportion like memory.

A cold summer breeze off the lake.

I carve a name into myself as if I were a tree.

Sometimes when I look just right I see a mountain in Minnesota. I rename the resort where we stayed. *The Missing Mountain Lodge of the North Sky.*

The pine trees stood by our cabin like the ancestors. In the night I could hear them whisper. Sometimes I could hear them talk to the wind. Sometimes I could almost hear them say who I was.

Greatgrandpa cut us off from knowing where we came from. But in those days you didn't hang around Indian Territory after you'd got in trouble.

Maybe I wouldn't have been here if he'd stayed in Indian Territory and kept his name.

It was the start of our migration north.

Each time I tell a story I tell it in a new way.

That's what history is.

You have all the possibilities you could become. Where would you go if you could drive? My father asked.

Nearly to Canada, I said.
The Arctic.

The North Star of the Sky.

I remember being in the backseat of my father's car. Maybe him saying something to my mother as we took off. Sometimes I felt nothing held us down.

Sometimes I call them back. Greatgrandpa Woods Lewis. Grandma Orvezene and Lewis, my father. I think when he died he headed north. Back to finish that vacation on Lake George. Still driving his car up there toward the North Star.

In my memory I'm gathering pebbles from the lake shore. Greatgrandpa and grandma looking over the edge of the sky. Their voices rolling like so many pebbles on the shore.

A Forecast of Snowfields, Wind

Ice chunks between cattails
and patches of brown grass.
One cloud in the pale sky.
A shed, boarded with shingles,
painted yellow.
Just keep going and going.
A scenery to get through.
The farm buildings,
the sky over the road,
sanded, plowed.
A bright red delivery truck
as if a toy from an old swayback barn.
The trail of a fencerow through the snow,
the large beetle of a snowmobile.
You think of it upsidedown,
its feelers whirring on the snowfields
streaked with wind,
the hayrolls of ice-fishing houses
on a frozen lake.

A Quick Rise from Icewater

The *lakeedge* scraped flat
under the plow of a glacier
until frozen over
you drive across it

but whatever's there
just *turnsover*
in the small boom-towns
of your breath

the large clouds
under the sky
the rough icefield
smaller away the higher *youget.*

An American Landscape

Years later a voice like hers
the whole scene returns
not clear but a radio program in the duplex
upstairs.

You know the steamheaters against the wall
like a row of old horsecollars.

It's her voice you hear
coming from the closet of your throat.

The woodwork on the wall
the floor and ceiling
heavy doorposts
cavetto moldings
carbels
cornices and newels
a loose rug running low under the window.

You think you want outside of what she was.
A trip to the North Shore
leaving the house closed up
a note in the milkbottle on the porch.
The still life of an American naturalist
on the wall.
The tinfoil of yellow twilight.

After a time you hear the silence
that fills the air.
The day has come to some light.
You think how all your life
your mother swept you away
cleaned bones and fragments of fur
tossing you into the nothingness
in which you planted your garden.

Sometimes you hear the cry of a landscape.
Sometimes you hear the scaffolding
of your bones.

A sudden rain when driving the highway.
But you get through quicker these moments
you can't see.

You don't want to come back
with a feeling of hurt to share.
You give nothing of yourself
because you unwrap the ghosts.

You know the words
every weight of them
mother and father
the same children coming up the street.

Someday you'll come to grips with yourself.
Meanwhile you tighten your arms.
You plug the channel of your ears
with a stick
and hear the words you carry silently
for years.

Now you dream you're levitating
only your feet drag.
Your mother is watching your shoes
scuff her floor.
She's wrapped in something like a cape
the way your child used to pin a towel
around his neck.
Finally you see she has wings.

You drop into the duplex against your wishes.
The two round cakes she just baked
watertowers on the edge of town.

Now you're driving the highway
and your mother flies over you.
Birds fill the air with birdnoise.
You could ask them to be quiet
but they're only passing

the way your children came and left
though they're coming up the street again
and you don't know what to do with them.

You want to work but your work doesn't come
for years.
You listen to their noise
scraping your thoughts.
The life you live on a back burner
will be yours again someday.

You hold that promise to your face
like a washcloth.
You say peace to the bathwater
its waves rising.
You say peace
while your mother floats over the cornices
cleaning her paws.

You praise the garden.
Your struggle up from it.
You cannot stop the gravity of words.
You feel the woo of earth
back down into itself.

Tattle

You remember those years running
unthreading
so as not to leave
a trail
so you wouldn't know
the terrible truth.
The awful plainness.
The hamfork.
Saying youcan't do anything
that matters
youknow you can't.
Dawn itself being
shuffed
down there
to another place
with it unnumbered
you run
trying to makeout.
You get into trouble
which is the first way.
Give yourself away
so there'll *beless* of you
to unravel.
Such resilience
You always thought it was
overeasy
the dull endurance of ordinarylife.

Ago

A sudden understanding of what
each one saying lines of however
they are told.

How do they reach
their expoundings
on a frozen lake to get across

scarring the surface
with something
like a hole for a line of fish?

A curtainfall underneath
the edge of little words like waves
delivered to the shore.

The Lines

Has anyone lain down here
beside those red peppers
or under those weak elm withers
standing in shame there?
"Lyric"
Gerald Stern

It's then you hear the lake shore
with its mouth open to the sky.
You know the clouds are white lids.
You see their isolation
yet they're a full source.

The waves go up like a wall
against the shore.
It must be where you float
between the conifers
each word you reach for swept away.

It's not anywhere you can lift off
the landscape
a transferable tracing
a more comprehensive given moment
you've already established.

It's why now when you're alone
you hear your lines again.

You know you return the offer
to forgive.
You hear the elm and garden
the praise of words they wait for.

You think a plane moves
over the clouds
that move over the earth.
For a moment you feel yourself rise.
You want a dreamlife among the angels
pushing your *part vision*

of the whole into the chinks.

You think it's too much,
this reunion to forgive.

Then over the red peppers
you lift your head.
You feel the backyard elm,
the grip of something
like a horsecollar.

You decide to speak
as if your part will last forever
in this temporary place
in which you live your life.

A Lake Swimming Beneath

Each ice-fishing house
a covering of drama

a call of gulls
from the easeful distance

the winter village overwater
an upsidedown gathering

on the closed door
of the lake.

Plane Window

The curly
lakeshore
winging
over west

a dome
of stone
on water

the brunted
stage
the lake
could take
lets once.

Dramatis

The characters don't actually live but someone maybe like them
the author knew and is grateful for somewhat writing down the
dialogue which travels from the stage picked up by a tailwind of
how lonely the characters on stage until conflict and resolution
with the other. The words memorized go back a little forward
without permanence but shifting. Beware of the edge they get near
as a plane window enveloping a dramatic scene. An unexpected
turn unlike the smooth-as-possible-for-passengers-paying. But
drama is turbulance. Not a flight without it yielding a wiser char-
acter with others rehearsing the scenes before the watch of oth-
ers. Now the excursion of curtains up and down. The reviewers
with a view. The gushers of performances strung like fish or a
line of tents on the prairie. The brief dinner rushing seatward in
their row a settlement of luggage a slight nudge to prose.

Obit

If I heard her she said
the woman was in
the Pacific
when her husband died
escaping the cold that
is our winter.
We are slow in taking
the opportunity to say
the right serves her justly
it travels under
any circumstance.
We should go no matter
what the risk.
The roof repaired
two years ago
still leaks
and we serve ourselves
and take the right to leave
past the winking bakery man
the row boat gunner
white caps
and all upon the water.
We row toward the Islands
hop a ship
when the right to leave
arises and we hope
forever to be there.

What's Your Story Seems to Be the Shade You're Under

You sit on the winter shore at Shovel Point
Palisades
on Lake Superior.
The waves crashing the rock.
Your ears open to space.
You could say you hear the spirits licking
the windowpane.
That heavy image of the sky
trumpting its last warming.
If you crease your eyes
you could see the spirits
in the frozen haze over Superior.
They're like birds near the folding chair.
Their fingers cold inside their mittens.
Their beaks with a wool scarf covering.
What's it like to sit at 12 below
before the waves the wind picks up like *fizz*?
You know that's what story is.
The lake shore thick with ice.
The waves answering the white chrysanthemums
curling from your breath.
You feel the air inside your nose.
You act as if you're in love with denial.
You can't be.
Not THAT cold.
No not that.

Actors

They are lined up on the map.
Their different topics last all winter.

They feel the mov't of water.
The birches on the shore rippling like waves.

A laugh. A cough.
Something they want to call *clapter.*

Boom Town

Actually you said nothing so long when you finally had a chance, it took a while to speak. And he who had something to say wouldn't. Taking it with him to the canoe dock across the lake that was supposed to be wrapped in white paper he brought from the stockyards for the venison. Sometimes he *rifled* in tirades or outbursts of anger. You still wear that costume crammed in a drawer so long the wrinkles never come out. Yet somehow you speak to the emptiness that moved on your plate between the potato mounds and venison. You even feel a setting of tents or buildings that might bloom into a town, or fold like a program, or start again in other places. You say your life may be a series of them. They listen to whatever you say from your place on the stage as you boast your short-lived drama. Your little boom-town life.

Front Rank

There's another
     way to

say this I'm
     sure but

to be blunt to
     say it

like it is
     the years

are an old
     record

collection
     left

in the back of
     the car

the volcanic
     burst

of family the
     wobbly

corridors of
     escape

it's when
     it all

blows past
     you hold

onto the laun-
     dry you

sweep the po-
        tatoes

you hit and
        watch

the homework
        go by

you wish it
        were

dearer it's
        why

you cry in
        front

of everyone
        when

you don't
        want to

spotting
        the card-

board covers
        that

hold the black
        disks

the tears that
        erode

the grooved
        fields

of your face
you lift

the basket of
sheets

you clothes-
pin

the shoulders
of your

blouse you
cling

to the faith
you'll get

through the
front

clothes line
you'll

be the one to
carry

the old warped
song.

Mostly It Was Arid There before the Windmill

Imagine a crucifix in the stairway
with spurs down the hall. The spurs turning
small windmills if you put your finger
to them. Imagine the crucifix over oldbodied

water in the horsetank. The spring winds
valleyward before boatery. Porticos flowing
with chiles. They came often to drink
on the plateau of the stairs. Rollable as

tumbleweed out of which a voice once spoke
humorless as the feet of a saint.
You might not want to waste your elbows on him
mostly varied now with the valley's decline.

But I say that human gusts of indifference
and derision don't mean anything there.
The gravity pulling it all ingrounded
so to speak. Sheets of dust

blowing off the old seabed. The eyes
uplifted from the crucifix in the stairway.
The spotted cowhide of a chair.
You see in the distance the turbulent

surface of humanity that passes there.
Imagine the spurs. The windmill jigging.
Imagine the propeller of an outboard motor
just before the cord is jerked.

Tableland

The snow's shriveled late March
to banks along the road.
Out here space's sectioned into chutes

and the sky drags its spurs against the land.
There're so many clouds
last winter some of them were pushed

out of the sky.
You hear the beginning of a story
over the checkered tablecloth of a cafe.

You see a sign, *Rodeo, Laramie.*
The slug of a truck coming uproad
across the back-prairie cut-off

loaded close under the sky.
You can't tell in the distance
if it's grazing herds or brush.

You feel old basins of lugwater
something to do
with leftovers surrounds you like the cold.

Riced Floors

This is not the end where it was supposed to come. The dwindling bluestem preserve. The prairie chickens on it. The sound of history in the few grasses left stirring one way then another making hairpin curves not seen until too late. They make a rooonng rooonng of their call. They stomp the land as if there's no place else they can go. They clear their throats. They raise the curtain as if it were the last place left.

Mt. Scott, Southwest Oklahoma

You have to have long feet to walk across the cattle-guard. A child couldn't. A buffalo or longhorn. Nor the bound feet of a woman. Now you follow the road through the wildlife refuge. At first, wind rakes dust across the road, and marsh-grasses ripple with waves. As you climb Mt. Scott on the old road, the lichen on granite boulders are kimono flowers. *2400 feet*, you say. *Not much.* But look at the yellowed prairie like a robe fallen on a floor and see a hundred miles crumpled in a hem. *Just feel* if you can, the kimono blowing open and this mountain, this bowed bone of one foot stepping.

Telegraph

Scissortails
    can't get

out of the way
    in time

5 a.m. highway
    212

South Dakota
    I'm on

the road
    couldn't

sleep with
    the way

ahead to go
    I'm alone

here I've
    always

known it
    but for

the Pentecostal
    Church

in the
    distance

a man on a
    horse

the land
    spread

under
the knife

of sky far
away the

Missouri River
you know

there'll be
a bridge

across it
somewhere

now I'm stopped
at a high-

way flagman
where I

had been making
time

a truckload
of it

and half the
boundary

speed goes by
with

the three
burrs

beside me on
the seat

I picked at
        Bear Butte

leaving a
        braid of

sweetgrass I
        traveled

with for miles
        hay-

loaves in
        fields

a loading
        chute

the highway
        under

construction
        I think

how even
        tongues

is a lonely
        language.

Kissing the Sun

The flowers of the prairie're saying
everywhere the hot sun straight up

is not the same that sets
in the evening

the singular workman dozing in his truck
is not the roadside marker

you want to stop at
the summerbaseball games

maybe between towns
the kids running to them

they pull buffalo skulls behind them
at sundances that dot the prairie

the skewers of elk bone under one's holy
loading of skin

is all you have of the careful rest
the *mana* you feel

enticing the heat
you taste the prairie

the sun the pole the bare
hot ball you know with your lips.

Wyoming

I'm driving on a road across Wyoming
I think of the man I left behind
to try this on my own
I've driven hundreds of miles
it's not like I'm by myself
I have memories
these tendernesses among
the highway markers
do you want a postcard
of my speedings
my notice at the edge of the sky
maybe our last wish is for loneliness
to drive these great distances
it's graceful to see the two of them
sky and earth
I think sometimes
the sky could drown in its ownness
without us
and the weather of the stars
downloads the plainness of the prairie
the sun fortunate as bees
will still be setting
while our migrations are over and remote
as highway 28
yet the motels are full of drama
consider this God
before you wipe out the world
with your dust cloth
love us a little longer
let us sing just one more song.

A Condensation during Flight

A rusted edge of the end is showing
your love says on returning
what's apparently the world
full of genocide
and inevitable deaths
what had to do with any of it
is what survived
with a longing cross
though not many know the lucid hope
or birds killed in the grill
or even a small car on a roadshow
it's the gushers of life
love
insight
sudden forgiveness
you remember fragile
as the civilization you've got here.

DIANE GLANCY is Associate Professor of English at Macalester College in St. Paul, Minnesota, where she teaches Native American Literature, Creative Writing and Scriptwriting. She received her B.A. from the University of Missouri and her M.F.A. from the University of Iowa.

She has received grants from the National Endowment for the Arts, the Minnesota State Arts Board and the Jerome Foundation.

Her anthologies include *Contemporary Plays by Women of Color*, edited by Kathy Perkins and Roberta Uno, Routledge, 1995; *Freeing the First Amendment, Critical Perspectives on Freedom of Expression*, edited by Robert Jensen and David Allen, New York University Press, 1995; *Writing Women's Lives, Autobiographical Narratives by Twentieth Century American Women Writers*, edited by Susan Cahill, Harper Perennial, New York, 1994; *The Norton Book of Science Fiction*, edited by Ursula K. Le Guin and Brian Attebery, W.W. Norton, New York, 1994; *The Pushcart Prize XVIII, Best of the Small Presses*, edited by Bill Henderson, Pushcart Press, Wainscott, New York, 1994; and *Two Worlds Walking* edited by Diane Glancy and Bill Truesdale, New Rivers Press, Minneapolis, 1994.

Her work is also mentioned in *What Is Found There, Essays on Poetry and Politics*, Adrienne Rich, W.W. Norton, New York, 1994.